HEART OF A DEER

PASCALE PETIT
Heart of a Deer

London
ENITHARMON PRESS
1998

First published in 1998
by the Enitharmon Press
36 St George's Avenue
London N7 0HD

Distributed in Europe
by Littlehampton Book Services
through Signature Book Representation
2 Little Peter Street
Manchester M15 4PS

Distributed in the USA and Canada
by Dufour Editions Inc.
PO Box 7, Chester Springs
PA 19425, USA

ISBN 1 900564 16 5

British Library Cataloguing-in-Publication Data.
A catalogue record for this book is available
from the British Library.

The Enitharmon Press gratefully acknowledges
a grant from the London Arts Board towards
the production costs of this book.

Set in 10pt Bembo by Bryan Williamson, Frome,
and printed in Great Britain by
The Cromwell Press, Wiltshire

In memory of my maternal grandmother

ACKNOWLEDGEMENTS

Acknowledgements are due to the editors of the following publications in which some of these poems first appeared: *Argotist*, *As Girls Could Boast* (Oscars Press 1994), *Beyond Bedlam* (Anvil 1997), *Exeter Poetry Prize* anthology (Odyssey Press 1996), *London Review of Books*, *Poetry Review*, *Poetry Wales*, *Quadrant* (Australia), *Risk Behaviour* and *Riding Pillion* (Smith/Doorstop Books 1993 and 1994), *Sheffield Thursday*, *South West Poetry Competition* anthologies (1991 and 1993), *Summoning the Sea* (University of Salzburg Press 1996), *The North*, *The Poet's Voice*, *The Rialto*, *Times Literary Supplement*, *Virago New Poets* (Virago Press 1993). An extract from 'The Book of Water' was displayed on London Buses in 1996-7 for Friends of the Earth's 25th anniversary.

A pamphlet collection of a number of these poems, *Icefall Climbing*, was published by Smith/Doorstop Books in 1994.

'Kanaima' won First Prize in the 1996 Sheffield Thursday Competition. 'The House of Shattering Light' won Third Prize in the 1996 Exeter Poetry Competition. 'Eisriesenwelt' won First Prize in the 1993 South West Poetry Competition.

I would like to thank Fray Cesáreo de Armellada (alias Emasensén Tuari) for his *Diccionario Pemón* and *Taurón Pantón, Pemontón Taremuru: Invocaciones mágicas de los Indios Pemón*, both invaluable sources for my poem 'Kanaima'. I would also like to thank Arnaldo Dugarte, my first guide in Auyan Tepuy and José Kumara, Atanasio Parkia and Juan Eimasensen for teaching me some Pemón and for their help in my second journey. 'Kanaima' is written in memory of Alexander Laime who lived on Little Rat Island then Orchid Island in the canyons of Auyan Tepuy for forty years and who died in 1994. I would like to acknowledge the influence of Joseph E. Rael's *Beautiful Painted Arrow* (Element 1992) on 'The House of Shattering Light' and 'As If I Were Winter Itself'; and Petru Popescu's *Amazon Beaming* (Abacus 1991) on 'The Book of Water' and 'The Book of Trees'.

CONTENTS

MIRADOR

When Gran fell downstairs and died I wanted to visit her house,
stand on top of the stairs and at the bottom
and on each step between her life and death.
I climbed carefully as once I'd climbed through cloud forest
over the tangle of roots on my way to see
Angel Falls from the mirador of Alexander Laime.

When I reached the lookout point where the whole cataract
can be viewed, sweat in my eyes and needle-fine spray,
there was drizzle, a driving wind,
dark clouds obscured the head of the falls.
For about a third of a mile up the amphitheatre
I saw how water after it has fallen so far
seems to flow back up then fall again
as air – spirals, comets, flames.

I thought of Jimmy Angel, discoverer of these falls,
how, after his death, his wife Marie
had a bush pilot fly her right up to the head
where sudden cloud can cause a crash.
And against the winds she opened the cockpit window
to throw his ashes, spray burning her face.
Then Laime the hermit built his hut on Rat Island
so he could watch dawn turn the plummeting waters to fire.

All night Gran was restless as rockets exploded
and fireworks lit up her uncurtained windows.
By four a.m. the ninety years of her life gathered forces
against the torrent that battered the panes.
Nine hundred metres to fall from the summit.
Bone and water, bone and air, the corridors
in sandstone where marrow has carved passages,
the base so strewn with rocks I could not see the plunge-pool.

But when I went and stood in Gran's hall, looking up
at the air that contained aftershocks and echoes,
the air I wanted to collect in boxes and label,
as I'd scooped the red soil at the foot of the falls
for proof of my visit, it was as if I was underwater,
all my childhood in her house falling on my head,
against my eyes, down my mouth, all the water and fire of my life.

GHOST LEAVES

They arrived mail order, twopence each,
enough to fill this box, to leaf one tree
– the sacred peepal, brother to the banyan,
a species of strangler fig with roots
that cling to the trunk of a host
forming an exoskeleton.

Also known as skeleton leaves.
Once dead, they fall with their veins
intact, the cellulose dried
to the colour of vellum. In India
they are used to paint miniatures
for weddings, funerals.

Scenes are depicted on a leaf shaped
like a heart, a thin dried heart
torn from its body with green blood
and green bloodcells which eat sunlight.
They lie in my box
eating the dark.

Their veins draw ghost-blood
from the great ghost-tree
also named the bodhi tree
where Gautama sat
and became Buddha, drawing enlightenment
from the green light of its leaves.

The stems encircled him
forming a lattice around his frame
– the matrix of an empty tree.
Forest denizens made short work of him.
Leaves sprouted from his bones.
An artist painted a thousand eyes on them.

He has been sitting for a thousand years
transforming light to oxygen.
Is Buddha in my box?
Is the hollow core of the peepal in my box?
If I unwound the ghost-veins of all these leaves
would they reach the sun?

But they are mooncoloured.
They give off a reflected glow like moonleaves.
They are eating moonlight to make airlessness.
They are making a moon atmosphere
here on earth, in my room, far from India.
Are the leaves cold, do they long for the rainforest,

their brothers and sisters, their extended families?
Have they been posted to the moon?
Can they hear the city outside my house?
The moonbox is in a room full of books.
Can they hear ancestors
buried in the books and wood of these shelves?

Is this the afterworld for forests?

THE HOUSE OF SHATTERING LIGHT

We house-hunted in marin country.
I was weak, so you fed me the hearts of deer.

Just beyond the dunes and before the scrub
we found the house of our dreams –

walls that retreated according to the moon,
floors that sprouted thorns when we quarrelled.

We discovered a secret room
where children were preparing themselves.

Some took out their eyes.
Some took off their noses, ears or legs
while some broke themselves exactly in half.

That night your snores quietened.
The truth butterflies flew out of your mouth.
My sweat pricked me like tiny needles,

my skin glowed with body lights.
I could see into my interior
as if gazing at a starry night.

I gathered the sweat from my skin,
poured it into this bottle,
labelled it The House of Shattering Light.

When I am homesick, I open the stopper.
At first, I smell a girl
with the heart of a deer.

When the blood-smell fades,
then, the waves of marin country
bring me the eyes, ears and legs of my babies.

MEMORIES OF A MARRIAGE

1. *Mr Baxter's Butterflies*

'Every collector dreads putting them to death'
he assured, opening the African cabinet.
'These are drawn to human sweat,
the excrement of leopards,
their beautiful or nauseous scents
are strongest when confined.

One fell prey to the robber-fly
which sucked its victim dry.
This white with six-inch wingspan
was borne on the wind like a letter.
My greatest find is a rare case
of Siamese twins, an eight-winged wonder.'

2. *Burning Beds*

Guillermo Kuitka said 'the bed is our first map'.
He painted sixty children's mattresses
with maps of countries we recognised,
warped by the topography of dreams.

Cities were buttons sunk in valleys.
Roads pierced teddy-bear patterns.
Rose designs wilted in yellow stains.
Sixty children's beds. No children.

3. *Burning Bed 37*

So this is where our eyes settled.
Hands explored homely contours
– the hills and plains of England.

Girl or boy? A toy railway.
A motorway leading to the edge of the dream
– the world was flat then, cities

were buttons to twirl around fingers.
And no matter how we slept,
the mattress refused to grow.

4. *The Imago*

In a suburb of London, Forest Gate
– the black birdwings of Borneo,
the moon-moth, the owl butterfly
with wings like three-dimensional dreams
of swooping, predatory eyes.

The mass migrations. A cloud
seeking a mate. Iridescent rain.
The forest they roosted on vanished
under a thousand wings; the trees dreaming.

Long after you left, I prised my box open,
feasted on foreign colour. As if
flakes of skin fallen through flocking
could be collected, I could now see,
at leisure, the finery of the male.

17

MY SON IS BEAUTIFUL AS THE SUN

(after a painting by Guillermo Kuitka)

His room is long and narrow,
brown as menstrual blood.
His bed-linen is purple.

Every morning I strip his bed.
I have painted a map on his mattress,
with legends of thorns, bones and syringes.

Highways are bloodlines
and land becomes skin –
a hundred miles to the inch.

By midday, I have gathered
the houseplants around his bed,
they are the forest he is lost in.

He sees my head above the fronds
as I pace from corner to corner
reading his last letter:

*Dear Ma, I am going into the Interior
to find the bird who wears a shield of sunrays.*

My Manakin, my Cock-of-the-Rock.
When I cough, his bird-plumes shrivel.

THE GHOST TRAP

1.

Even their names sound like departures
– the ghost moth, scarce vapourer.

Their worms feed while I sleep.
Miners, millers, gall makers.
Caterpillars with oddly shaped bodies,

outgrowths of clubs, horns, spurs,
legs that have hooks and crochets,
trail streets of silk, ladders.

When I hear those high-pitched squeaks
I go out into the garden
where white cocoons are draped:

boat-shaped, earthen, mummyform
or flimsy as shreds of wedding veil,
some in underground burrows

others airborne, but safe in their tents of leaves,
the threads interwoven
with stinging hairs from their bodies.

Discreetly as moonlight in sunlight –
one worm adds clay to her cell,
another, chewed wood, building a robust shelter.

2.

Since you've gone, I've become nocturnal,
hovering in the shade of my back door
while the ultraviolet lamp draws them into my sheet.

I also bait with beer-soaked fruit
or scraps of rotting meat
then transfer them to the killing bottle.

If death is too slow, they tear their wings
so I use cyanide in a range of bottles
for the small and minute moths.

Larger males are injected in the thorax
through a syringe or sewing-machine needle,
its eye loaded with deadly fluid.

I pin them before they're dead,
keep them damp, so I can set the wings
without having to relax them.

Then I label —
their name, family and details
concerning capture.

AMONG THE SEQUOIAS

The National Park guard takes my fee

then I'm alone in the great forest,
among giant trees with men's names.

This is how it will be –
me cutting a shirt of fibrous bark

pretending I'm tall,
trying to get acquainted,

get their measure – height,
girth, tonnage, age;

while they just stand there,
roots thicker than my waist,

joined underground
in a vast, silent, system.

WHAT SHE WANTED

What she wanted was to return
to the original rainforest

hear water pushing
through the sapwood

and leaves eating light
as she wanted to eat light.

She knew her nature
was to be water, not wood.

She knew there was a grove
of vertical rivers

of roaring waterfall-trees,
and a grove of whirlpool-trees

with vortices she could dive through,
past the hollow years of her life

right back to the roots.

ANGEL FALLS IN LOVE

Nobody had seen a waterfall so high. He thought
I was the last thing people see when they die.

His plane rose vertically until it reached the dot
my three-thousand-foot fall pours out of.
Then he crash-landed on my mountain
and called it Devil's Mountain.

He stood over me and shouted his name – Angel,
Jimmy Angel. I think he married me because
he gave me his name. All I'd known was this
hot stone that rises out of the clouds into thin air.
His eyes were blue as this sky. In them I saw myself,

two selves in his sunglasses. He kissed me.
He leant over the precipice and drenched his face,
couldn't get close enough. He must have been wondering
how the hell he could escape, back to his kind.

Since then, there's been the rare visitor.
Once, a film crew appeared to make *The Lost World*
and I swayed, danced for them, I roared, I sang,
making my debut to the rest of the earth.
Then they left, and there was this silence.

WATERFALL CLIMBING

Some men are climbing up me.
I am stuck on this alp
which is as hard and solid
as the memory of my marriage.
I can't get out of this dress
now that the ice has bound my limbs.
Have they come to help?
They do not talk to me.
I don't think they even notice
that they are clinging to a bride.
One of them is hanging from my hem.
Another is perched on one of my breasts.
The third is sticking his ice-pick
into my thigh. He levers himself up.
A fourth is crawling over my veil,
embedding a crampon in my cheek.
One wrong blow, and I would crumple,
the silk is rotten in places.
It's not often men can climb all over me.
The conditions have to be just right.
A day too late, and I'd thaw, escape.
They are shouting back and forth.
Their calls start mini-avalanches.
They are too close to see who I am,
how beautiful I look on this my royal day,
imprisoned like a cake in layers of icing.
They complain I give them frost-nip.
Their gloved fingers are rough.
They think nothing of staring
through my petticoats and lingerie
in to my white bones
and the black cave beyond.
They hack and hack at loose hair.
Then the boldest hauls himself
over my forehead, crows to his mates.

All along they were joined
by the rope of friendship.
They go home, now that I am conquered,
back to their wives and children.

THE CACHAMAY RAPIDS

The clouds are so heavy they touch the water.
They are full of words, tropical storms of words
about to burst, held in for the moment.

At the stern lies the bucket for bailing out.
At the helm, a guide peers at his script.
He starts by describing the Orinoco,
a benign, whitewater river

but we are not on the Orinoco,
we are on the Caroni, which is black.
For miles the two flowed side by side
without mingling. The rain smudges his notes.

The river is so wide I can't see the banks.
The Cachamay rapids fill the horizon.
I have always lived in a torrent.
I don't hear the thunder anymore.

I've passed into its heart, where there are
rooms of white silence, rooms of black silence.

IGUAÇU FALLS, BRAZIL

This time, as we enter the canyon,
we try to drown the voices in Rio
where the president is talking too loud.

We were the sweat
on the arm of the soldier
who shot a child

to clean up the streets of One World City.
And we were the fear
that ran down the child's leg.

We have been the leaves
of an unknown species
which could have cured cancer.

All is calm in One World City
where the Ones Who Work Slowly
are sleeping off lunch.

Can't they hear our earth-shaking thunder?
We are holding our own Summit
in the Cascades, in the Ravine.

We are talking fast as possible
in the mighty Iguaçu
where thirty rivers meet.

We are chanting our moon-names –
Crises, Ocean of Storms, Marsh of Decay,
Sea of Tears. We are in our flood-month.

You call us the Devil's Throat.
You pay the boatman
to take you to Trembling Island.

You ride a jeep through
raucous forest, where we are
flowers, birds, butterflies, snakes.

You stare right into our jaws
as we shout our own treaty
on biodiversity

using our moon-names –
Fertility, Bay of Rainbows,
Sea of Rains, Lake of Dreams.

THE REMEMBERING ROOM

She plays *Rainforest Requiem* at full volume,
rewinding side B: noon to nightfall,

kicked off by the screaming piha's whistle
then the cacique's alarm as the first

thunder-rolls bounce off bedroom walls.
The macaws' flight signals the first drops.

She slows, comes to a standstill,
eyes scanning the ceiling for lightning.

The recorded rain falls faster, harder,
until she's clean as a blank map.

She starts repainting her room
– everything white, including windows.

No one will find their way in,
not even the poisonous streetlight.

She's invisible as the musician wren
which sings a duet with her

from the impenetrable thicket.
Together, once again, they paint out the night.

THE WEIGHT OF LIGHT

All day I searched
for leaves that were falling
but had not touched the ground.

In memory of the canopy
I overlap them,
moongreen on sungreen
stitched together with thorns

to make a sleeping-bag
of leaves from the last forest.

I lie in this bed
for only one night

under the tree
with skins draped from its branches,
the fungus-eared listening tree,

my face exposed to moonburn,
the skin of my face
grazed by lightfish in rivers of moonlight.

Their scales are mirrors
held against my eyes.

My eyelids try to grow bark
to shield me from thunder stones
and dust that is earth's pollen.

Then the orioles settle on the fungus-eared tree
and sing while they turn
the skins into hanging nests,

all night they work
weaving ribbons of moonlight into long purses,
then lay their eggs heavy as worlds.

THE HUMMINGBIRDS OF VENEZUELA

Waking in the small hours
from another dream of the Lost World
I search my Schauensee guide

for Singing Assemblies of Hairy Hermits,
Sunangels, Woodstars, Flowerpiercers
and all your spirit names.

With bills long enough
to draw hallucinogens
from the trumpets of daturas

you are rufous-shafted,
gorgeted, violet-eared.
A soft whistle, a series of peeps, a churr

and I see your shot-silk colours:
coppery-purple, ruby-topaz,
ochraceous Moonangels.

Inhabitants of the lofty tepuis
and deep simas, from Orchid Island
to the slopes of Misty Mountain

you suspend your havens
of rootlets and lichens,
bound with cobweb and palm fibre.

Deeply forked, spangled Coquettes.
Pollinators of my dreams.
Companions through my coldest nights.

TRANS AMAZON HIGHWAY

After the cloudburst, everything is silver,
flashes under our four-wheel-drive.
I've counted seven corpses of dogs,
one anteater, a jaguar

and a boa threshing across the road,
its head run over by a truck
while we are crushing its lower spine,

as if a cloud-snake had fallen from heaven.

CLOUD FOREST

To enter the forest
with leaves falling like rain,

wear a veil of many webs,
some so musty you are invisible.

You must smell of mould. Dress
in a patchwork of petals or butterfly scales.

Remove the soles from your store-bought shoes,
replace them with skin from a sloth

so you can hang upside-down
from the ghost-branches,

crawl slowly backwards through time.
Or paint your palms with beetle-blood,

bore to the heartwood
through cracks crooked as lightning.

There is nowhere left to go
but into yourself. You recognise organs

like landmarks, scars between the years.
You are learning to touch the curves

of immense rings, entering the age
when leaves converted air to light,

the forest glowing in the dark
like an X-ray of a lung.

Rest against the buttress of a tree
with its crown in the house of thunder.

Remember rooms lined with pollen
and the down of nestlings,

the nursery where children
tore leaves along their veins,

the fragments kept for birthdays,
games with the magnifying-glass.

To quench your thirst,
drink the mirrored clouds from the rivers.

Then a silence will fall
like soft dust from the stars.

THE BOOK OF TREES

I was in a floatplane, searching for a clear stretch
on the Javari river, then among the words.
Consonants towered above me blocking out the light.
I'd brought some gifts which I left on the riverbank
to lure a tribe never contacted by whites.
Soon I was following them into the Amazon.
We weaved through chapters tangled with lianas.

I could not speak to the Mayoruna
but their shaman planted thoughts in my head
which grew in my own language.
They were retreating to the beginning of time.
The girls were secluded for puberty rites.
The women burnt their belongings, their dead,
they could not take them back to their past.

The pages steepened. Then we were above the treeline.
By day the pages had layers of dense sentences.
When night fell I could see nothing. I had to feel my way
through this part of the book. I learnt that one darkness
is rough, another smooth, yet another has thorns.
I learnt to read with all my nerve-endings.
I chewed manioc, sucked the venom from frogs' sacs.

I saw the twin waterfall at the source of the Javari
and the mountain which must not be viewed directly.
Morpho butterflies, with sky-blue wings and night-black
undersides, emerged from the cocoons of those words.
Then it rained harder than I have ever known rain,
forcing us downriver. I was swept from the end of the story
back to the beginning. I cannot get out of this book.
              I have been changed by it as air is changed
              when it passes through the pores of a leaf.

DRESSING THE MOUNTAINS

I filled my rooms with rubbish
picked up from the streets –
shopping lists, broken settees,
and while car-seats and planks
held back the walls of my hungry home
I composed a Dressing Chant,
not from precious stones and pollens
but from the dust and debris in drawers.

From beads, buttons, car-oil and wire-wool
I gathered a cloud of black pollen. Male rain.
From painkillers, dried milk and confetti
I gathered a cloud of white seeds. Female rain.
My voice reached the first slope, summoning a squall.
Over a pile of anonymous photos
I set snares made from my own hair
to catch birds blown in from their course.

With party glitter, hundreds and thousands,
I drew sun-circles on the right side of my body,
moon-circles on the left.
I placed my right foot on the black pollen footprint,
my left on the white seed print.
The Navaho say each mountain
must contain a child to be whole,
it isn't enough to be a spirit.

Into the Sleeping Mountain I dragged
a mattress retrieved from the skip.
I tied men's clothes together for a man-shape,
fleshed him with snail shells, junk mail.
I tied women's clothes together for a woman-shape,
fleshed her with plant pots, bin bags.
They were the first man and woman
whispering in their hogan.

I named my sitting-room Sitting Mountain,
placed the Dawn Boy inside.
I made him from faded curtains, a toy phone
that rings when I move him.
I named my kitchen Eating Mountain,
placed the Twilight Girl inside,
made her from cracked plates, empty washing-up bottles
that whistle when I squeeze her.

THE BUTTERFLY HOUSE

After a year of illness, I went
to the tropical butterfly house, passed
through the door protected by flaps;
but they settled on my clothes,
I had to move carefully, and if
my neck tickled, remember not to scratch.

Something gave under my foot – the birdwing
looked uninjured, no tear or ooze of white blood
but the wound could be internal,
the notice said some lived only one day
while heliconids could draw protein
from pollen, live a full eight months.

The emerging cages were set back:
row on row of chrysalids glued to sticks
– bronze, lemon, green, iridescent,
spined like ghost murexes, with metal seals.
The Indian leaf pupa was shaped like a dead leaf.
Others could have been lunar leaves, star-scrolls.

They were opening faster now the sun had come out.
They were like good and bad days
lined up on the bars of my bed,
when all I could do was wait
to see how the best might dry out,
knowing that some would taste
bitter as the bile I'd kept vomiting.

I retreated to a bench in the corner
to study each specimen
as if constructing a patchwork skin;
scanned the butterfly guide for names,
as once I'd emerged from the anaesthetic
checking each part was still in place,
the nerves of my body alert and flying.

It was then I saw the great owl butterfly:
Caligo memnon – not just owl-eyed
but with scales mimicking face-feathers
and all this on the underside.
I too could be both prey and predator,
my stitches tight as an owl's talons
under my dressings, now that I was tired.

At the exit I inspected my clothes
as requested, until a clear-wings appeared
and I had to go back to see these miniature
windows with their stained-glass tips,
the imago house no human
would ever be light enough to enter.
Then I really did leave. I shook myself free.

KANAIMA

Kanaimaton piak ete se — we are in Kanaima's house.

The clouds float by like hungry continents.
Even water needs to eat.
The nature of water is muscular.

It was in an unpapered room I began to dream.
I spoke a secret language: *itei* — savanna
tureta — forest, *walpi* — night, *pena* — time past.

My father's name was *Kanaima* — devil-of-the-dark,
his house Devil Mountain, many-corridored.
Etamen waki — may you walk well!

In a northern city, the boards were bare.
They buckled beneath me like world rivers
laid side by side, nailed down.

Marooned on the sky-island of my bed
I called to the past and future
for a strong young guide.

Kanaima, Spirit of Tobacco, of Cachiri beer,
the wall dividing your room and mine
was made of crates. The beer-bottles spoke

in the *walpi* dark, the air many-limbed.
Night coiled around me like the legs of a lover.
The Tobacco Spirit crept into my room

through cracks between the crates. The last
murmurs of thunder clung to the ceiling
above which sky-people paced . . .

That morning, I saw a youth float downcurrent
on a raft, his skin gold-dusted.

Atimboro auti – where are you going?

I embarked on a journey.

Tukui the flowerpiercer
and Aruka the torrent-tyrant
protected me from Kanaima.

He came disguised as a great butterfly
his wings like maps
with legends of false eyes.

I knew him by the odour of his body.

Tukui and Aruka pecked his wings
just as he was sipping the Cachiri dregs.

My hammock scorched.

The moon smelt of old shoes and garbage.

After hours of scraping my elbows against bark
a ceiling of clouds opened.

By reciting names of hummingbirds
I survived Tears Crossing,
its spray sharp as the bills
of sunangels, woodjewels.

Then found the nest of a king vulture.

Balancing boulders marked the summit.

Kumara lit a fire, began to chant:
'Kanaima – father-of-the-forest . . .'

I longed for the comfort of Canaima Camp,
the smells from its restaurant
and sounds from a five star lagoon
where shadows dived into whirlpools

and a gold youth appeared once
on a raft of thunder
bearing the wealth of the Amazon.

Pata – world, *katurui* – saliva-of-the-stars.

'At that time, the forest was in the sky.
The stars were our birds. They sang
incantations against Kanaima.'

Kumara inspected my Schauensee guide,
stroked the illustration of a bellbird

then turned to his Cosmopolitan,
tried to read an advert.
Girls with skins like moonlight.

Back at Orchid Island, weaver–birds
had nested in my garden:
densely braided globes
safer than my hut
that admitted bird–eating spiders.

Kumara continued downriver
– a waiter at Canaima Hotel
where gringas ordered cocktails.

Soon, he'd return with phrases
in his notebook for me to interpret.

We traded language.
He taught me the piasan invocations,

stars low enough to talk to.
I'd learn their names,

how to find the leaf to calm storms,
the cure for homesickness.

'*Mu* – son, semen, root of the bitter manioc,
we Pemón are poor but rich in *taren*.
It's unwise, even for an Ingleshpon
not to know some spells in the forest.'

I worked on my maps, heartened
by Kumara's voice on my recorder.

Not a voice from the tree
that had sprung up overnight,
whose seeds grew into ghosts
that slung their hammocks in my chest.

A black biting mist hung over the island.

The clouds leant their stomachs against my roof.

I blew the dust from Devil's Canyon,
placed my model of Wei Tepuy at the entrance
to guard the heart-shaped mountain –
a world that so enchanted me I could not leave.

'*Iroma* – breath-of-life, laughter,
the wind music heard on top of the tepuy.'

In the sky-room a fog descended.
Father showed me his collection of morphos
'caught by flashing mirrors
as decoys, to trap a mate'.

His hands were lightning-blue
from stroking their scales,
they settled on my face
like a butterfly drinking liquor

then flew away, never to drink me again.
I made myself sweet as rotting fruit.
I hunted those sky-blue wings,
dustmotes of Father's attic,
dusted my face with them to climb the plateau.

Kumara, who had guided me
to Matawi Tepuy – Suicide Mountain,
refused to set foot in the devil's house.

Nor would he look at the shining blue face
of the sky-goddess.
He shrank from my blue fingers,
the false eyes painted on my palms,
my necklace of abdomens pierced by pins.

There are no words in English or Pemón
to describe the wings of the emperor morpho.
Encircled in a cloud of males
I climbed the rose-red cliffs.

The fog was a rag stuffed in my mouth.

Clouds smelling of formaldehyde,
dead clouds, grey wings of used morphos,
their scales stripped, exposing sky veins.

Days preserved like butterflies in drawers,
cabinets of unopened years,
a store-room, a loft, an unlived life.

The campbed which should have been
'a hammock woven from your mother's hair
to protect you from Kanaima'.

His eyes behind glasses
like rooms behind windows, false rooms,
me in a sky-house;
a man, a fog, the taste of mothball,

men in the courtyard
casting shadows across my wall,
footsteps, a bin-lid dropped
on the cobbles of Devil's Canyon.

A storm blew in through the broken window,
tore wings from bodies, words from mouths,
brought the outside in, the inside out;
flying rooms that settled on this plateau.

He used to blow smoke-rings around me
while he admired his morphos,
the Father of Ferocity, Father of Flint,
Home–Demolisher, Door–Slammer.

When I say silence, he is quiet.

The eyespots of the emperor morpho
are named Whirlwind, Old Woman's Clitoris.

How cold they must have been,
those angels, in England,
reflecting light from stars.

Kiamenti, uru – moondust, sundust,
the corridors of Kanaima's house
contained clouds of dust.

Concealed in a grey cocoon
I grew a blue starskin.

The sunrays Seterima, Uruturu,
appeared like smiles on a clouded face.

I squeezed between a jumble of rocks
shaped like Father's cars,
through a crash, a dump

to the Swamp that might devour
me if I caused rain

or angered the winds.
They crouched at the corners of his house
and could be raised by a wrong thought.

The worst storms are silent.
After rooms of repressed thunder:

the Valley of Stone Penises.

Followed by the Valley of Stone Children
who have grown algal skins.

The winds carved holes through them
to make wind music.

The sky was a playground for sky-children.
A group of clouds played tag.
A gang of clouds linked hands
around a cloud from another sky,
making it race with them.

I felt *konok* – drizzle
from the Iguana Constellation.

I struggled over house-sized boulders
towards a tower with ledges and overhangs,
named my shelter after a hotel Father had stayed in.

From my eyrie I saw distant tepuyes
rise like islands from the mist.

As night fell, the lights of Canaima Camp
blinked across the Gran Sabana.

The rocks moved at twilight,
re-arranged themselves
into ruins of the past and future:
quartz cities with crystal corridors,
rain-rooms with forests for furniture.

In Kanaima's hotel, I heard laughter
from rooms packed with men,
great gambling dens,
bars I could not enter,
lined with precious gems.

Men with solid gold bodies
were drinking and smoking,
talking loud as thunder.

All night the hotel shook
as I eavesdropped on my father.

The white music was heavenly,
Kumara could listen to it all evening,
weaving between tables, half-remembering
the steps of the old Tukui dance.

The customers were Kanaimaton.
They brought the silver sickness to his rivers.
Later, he'd write their names on leaves,
feed them to the roots of the Wadaka Tree.

Darkness crept up the rock wall.
But in Canaima Hotel it was always light,
the guests ready for the night's entertainment.

He went home and applied oil, then pollen
gathered from the slopes of Sun Mountain,
gilded his skin for a night on the river.

Emarima tuna – I wanted to marry the river,
to take, as husband, a boatman
who could steer by starlight

between rocks familiar as his knuckles,
to watch currents interweave
like the muscles on his arms . . .

'*Aten poino* — where have you been?' he asked.

I have been lost in the forest.
I have been walking in the dark.

I have been the butterfly Avakaparu
sucking the sap of injured trees.

Tukui and Aruka murmured *tu-itu*.

I was flying in my sleep
along the flanks of Auyantepuy

towards a blue light on the sand.

Papai was flashing a mirror
which became a door as I landed.
I woke in a smoky hut.

They gave me a drunkard's vomit
and when I got drunk on a tiny sip
they said she is Kanaima's daughter.

'What did you find on the summit?'

I went to ask Kanaima a question:
Ay-enchi kanan – do you have a daughter?

There was silence. The clouds were cotton wool
Father used to wrap his morphos in.

When does dew become dust, or a day die?

The night of the great storm
I climbed down a ladder of lightning
to ghost-trees trailing sleeves of lichen.

New islands were launched into the sky.
They crashed to the canyon floor
tearing holes in the canopy.

Just as a sapling suddenly flourishes
from a new source of light, so a memory
grew fresh shoots, became an emergent tree.

The first time my door opened
there was music, dancing,
Father carried me among the lights.

The next time my door opened
a strange man swept me in his arms
crying 'My daughter, my daughter'.

The third time my door opened
a hummingbird flew in
singing spells against Kanaima.

I entered the Great Northern Labyrinth
just as the sun was rising.
Rays pierced the mist, lit quartz formations.

The giant wings of a stone butterfly
dazzled me with crystal scales.

Each rainy season I return
to search for that vision.
Even when I sleep, the wings are above me,
casting prisms across my face.

During the dry months, I work on my maps.

Kumara has long gone.
I play his voice on my recorder.

On golden days, a male morpho
visits my hut
flapping his wings lazily.

I offer him a drop of Cachiri
and we both doze in the heat.

Notes

tepuy   — table mountain, house, house of the gods. These formations are found mostly in the Gran Sabana region of S.E. Venezuela and are some of the oldest rocks on earth.

Auyan Tepuy   — Devil's Mountain or House of the God of Evil. The largest tepuy with 700 square kilometres. It is almost divided by Devil's Canyon.

Wei Tepuy   — Sun Mountain. Sun and Moon Mountains are at the entrance to Devil's Canyon and are considered sacred by the Pemón Indians of the area.

Wadaka Tree   — Tree of Life or Tree of Many Fruits. A legendary stone tree near Mt. Roraima.

taren   — does not really translate. Approximately: magical invocations.

Pronunciation Guide

In Pemón the stress usually falls on the last syllable of a word e.g. iroma

Kanaima	—	Kan eye ma
pena	—	p ay na
auti	—	ow tee
Auyan Tepuy	—	ow yan te pooy
Uruturu	—	oo roo too roo
poino	—	p oy no

EISRIESENWELT

Eisriesenwelt — the Ice Giants' World, is the largest ice-cave in the world, high in the Austrian Alps. It is full of ice-formations such as the Icewall and the Icedoor.

In the world of the ice giants
I'm not afraid.

Today, I glided into the cave.
I wore glass shoes.

When I held my hand
against the light

I could see the veins
tunnelling through my palm

like a system of caves.
I stripped,

so the ice could fill me.

★

When I left home
I sculpted my parents in ice
but they kept melting.
The tutors complained.
They said water was formless.
I needed a fridge large as Eisriesenwelt,
26 miles long, to store my art.

So I tried glass.
Sometimes I touch the ice
and think it's fire –
the white heat of the kiln
where glass sculptures are cast.
I tried to rebuild my grandmother's greenhouse.
I made glass trees, glass rain, and a glass grandmother,

but they annealed too fast. They cracked.

★

Welcome to my studio
full of figures and towers.
Some of the towers are people.
Some of the people are towers.

Don't blame the artist.
I make what the ice-giants dictate.
If they say *stay in the studio overnight*,
I stay.

They made me carve
a stone dress for my mother.
I am not to blame
for its weight.

I was the lacemaker
who used frost
instead of silk
for her underclothes.

★

I created an entire wardrobe –

a dress of green ice
for my mother the sea,

a dress of blue ice
for my mother the sky,

a dress of black ice
for my mother the earth.

Her body shone through the green dress
like a reef.

Her body shone through the blue dress
like the sun.

Her body shone through the black dress
like a corpse.

My hands were raw from sewing
molten gossamers of spun glass

which shattered
when worn.

She was a tower of broken windows.

★

My mother has put all her clothes on,
armouring herself against me.
If I ask the right question
one of the dresses will answer.
They speak different languages.
There is the language of glass –
window-glass and lead-crystal,
and the language of ice –
blue, green and black ice.

She leads me to a house
where I spend five years
surrounded by emerald and ruby tears,
by turquoise and sapphire tears.
She has shed so many jewels
they form seas in our rooms.
I call my mother's seas
Sea of Sadness, the Bitter Sea,
Sea of Madness, the Guilty Sea.

★

Welcome to our sitting room.
It's hard to cross it, so we don't.

We're those two
facing each other across the ice.

The walls are furred.
My mother is waiting for me to defrost them.

Long blue icicles hang from the ceiling
like rain from a permanent storm.

Even in caves, wind can blow out light.
The draught has plunged us into darkness.

My mother's tears freeze. They fall
onto her body like stitches in a glass dress

knitted from the seas of her sadness.
Dresses within dresses. Mothers within daughters.

Because I am young. Because I am alive,
the Icedoor is open. I remember

we passed it before the fridge took over.
Perhaps on a postcard, in a letter.

60

It was a mouth. My mouth.
I said yes. I'll visit. Every weekend.

Yes. I'll come back, defrosting,
cleaning the scraps from the shelves.

Mow the lawn. Mow the mountains of Austria.

I got up. I slipped. I crawled along the floor.
Down frozen waterfalls I slid. Down the Icewall.

The cable-car was waiting for me.

The inn was warm. My life was warm.

AS IF I WERE WINTER ITSELF

When I enter the hospital where my mother is lying

I will bring a flask of water collected from Lethe
and a flask from the Mnemosyne.

I will sip from each.
This will feel like swallowing shafts of sunlight.

I'll take deep breaths, hungry for canyon air.

A porter will rub fox-fire on my face
for the ride in the luminous lift.

Corridor walls will be translucent,
I'll see the trees imprisoned inside –

blue branches with old wounds as leaves,
red trees with raptor-roots.

Are you ready for the truth?

Ward Sister will ask, releasing
lemon–yellow and saffron butterflies.

They are the first flurry of winter
I'll reply, addressing

Mother's forgetting eye
and her remembering eye.

Then I'll say everything I always wanted to say to her.

The butterflies will mass on her bed,

rays streaming through the window
will wash us both.

Her hands will shake but that won't stop me.

MY MOTHER'S CLOTHES

The air was full of Gitane Filtre, her reflection

transformed by the spray that lifts from torrents,
the wardrobe door open, her clothes pristine.

Some were in polythene, preserved in the mist
from the day they were worn; a blue and peach suit

striped with Iceland's primeval landscape
where fire and ice hiss under Northern Lights.

She told me about her year in the Indian Embassy,
unwrapped a sari deep as the Gokak Falls,

charged with rust-red debris. Its many mirrors
retained faces of her admirers.

Right at the back, trailing along the wardrobe floor,
her bridal-dress was a river shot with scales of salmon.

Next were négligés, subterranean springs
cascading down slopes of mountains,

then a dressing-gown which towered in the frosty depths,
its cataract of ice fastening at her throat;

an emerald trouser-suit with matching silk blouse
was a secret chute from the South of France

where she'd tried to make us a home.
I fondled the ruff, its underwood trickle.

After that, there were no more choice materials,
only dull tweeds, sober crêpes for the mature woman,

modest falls in the Welsh hills where she'd settled.

MY MOTHER'S HAIR

A cataract crashed on Mother's shoulder, was lifted,
plunged down her back. I clung to the armchair,

wanted to know where it all came from, the source
of rivers, whirlpools, which were driven by her brush.

I saw the blue lightning inside auburn shafts,
the transformation from water into harnessed power.

Frost came from a spray-can. She pressed the nozzle
and out flew blizzards, freezing curls as they sparked.

FROZEN FALLS

We are the frozen people,
the subhuman, misshaped people.

We'd like to throw ourselves
into the river, merge with the sea

but our parents
were winds

which slapped our cheeks
until they went numb.

We're so thin
we're transparent.

We are too tall,
elongated by icicles.

Some of us don't have faces.
Some of us have clothes but no bodies.

We hang from the rail
waiting to be worn.

We have ethereal names –
Fallen Angel,

Bridalveil,
Virgin's Tears . . .

THE FROZEN WATERFALL

After I climbed the long twisted braids
white as my grandmother's hair
I was tired. I felt old.
My clothes were in the way
so I removed them.
I didn't feel cold.

The frost entered each cell like a girl
who no longer cares where she sleeps.
The frost entered my cells like a cinema.
The film is set in Norway.
There is no beginning. No end.
Whoever enters, comes in halfway.

The frost entered my veins like a commuter
in a capital city, along escalators, lifts,
entered my heart like a customer
in a store where rain is for sale,
rainbows are for sale, and there are
waterfalls rolled on the shelves, like lace.

It is Christmas, a wedding
and a birthday, so everything must be sold.
The colours of my body must be sold,
the smells, the dark (must be made light),
the warmth, which is very expensive,
must go, and will be exchanged

for a currency of stars, silver coins
that are moons, gold coins that are suns.
The universe would sell its space
for my endangered blood
– afloat in a globe of water
which has not yet frozen.

The frost stares out of my pores
as if out of hospital windows,
turns to the wall, where a frozen waterfall
hangs in lucid precision. Each pennant
is a pain, and will not thaw.
The icicles hang down like sheets
from a bed which has been tipped upwards.

ICEFALL CLIMBING IN TIBET I

I am facing the icefall at the base of Everest.
A great white city is slowly subsiding.
The walls are never the same, never quiet.
An avalanche lands with a suppressed sigh.
I put on my crampons, sharpen my axe,
pass through the gate, which collapses after me.
Some of the rooms have crumbled. Some are lit
by the blue and pink lamps of my mother's house.
I wipe the window which reveals our lounge.
Mother is rocking. Her rhythm drives the city
over the cliff. Her rhythm keeps her warm.
She is knitting me a cardigan white as snow.
Her eyes are the windows of a deserted home.
I tap on the ice, but she can't see. I want
to ask her why she settled here, her dream
of travelling to Tibet, to religious air.
Her chair begins to melt, and I am scratching
at ice packed in annual layers which recede
to the beginning of time. A wall topples,
but I have arrived, and I will go on,
digging my spikes into a vertical façade
until I reach a bedroom window, the master-bed
with no master, the mistress of the house, ill.

There is a blue lampshade on the bedside table
and a dressing-table with the towers and domes
of my mother's make-up, perfumes, jewellery box.
A powder-puff lies abandoned, the powder spilt.
My mother's face is blue. She is lying under the quilt
which she made, sewing the patches of her life
into a stained glass mosaic, over the church of her body.
I am bending over her with a cup of tea, a bunch of flowers,
a loveletter, breakfast. She wakes. She eats. She
gets better. She moves house. I want to carry her away,
but the city is groaning. Crowds swarm the streets
then are buried alive. Other windows are atriums.

In them are forests. There are riots. Cars are smashed.
An axe breaks the plate-glass and trees wither.
The city is shaking under the stampede of my family.
Parts form meltwaters. A bridge sinks into a river.
I recognise Paris, London. I have lived in both.
I see myself as a child playing under the Eiffel Tower,
then as an adult, living near Alexandra Palace
the day it caught fire. The exits have caved in.
There is nothing I can do but take a room and live here.

ICEFALL CLIMBING IN TIBET II

Every adventurer has heard of the great white city
which is the gateway to Everest. It is fed
by the Khumbu glacier, only to collapse over
a cliff, in a series of seracs the size of hotels.
The city wants citizens. There are rooms to let.
When the sun shines, cracks gape in the pavement,
claim the most seasoned climber. I must concentrate.

My crampon spikes must match the rungs of the ladder
propped over a crevasse. I am enclosed in the womb
of my headlamp, climbing by night, when the temperature
isn't so high that the ice thaws, isn't so low
that it snows. One snowflake is nothing in itself,
a cold word softly slipped in conversation. Larger flakes
sting the cheek. A snowstorm caused the avalanche
which buried my friend. I try not to think of his
deepfrozen body encased above previous corpses.
I am alert to the tremors of distant icequakes,
their effect on houses precariously balanced.

Like all such capitals, constantly rebuilt
with haphazard streets, there is an old quarter.
In the centre of the icefall, the buildings are blue.
Time is measured in annual bands. Rooms are packed
with records of past generations. The ice preserves
each birth, each orgasm, each death. The ice
groans so much I think I'm in a hospital. Everyone
is wearing white. There are wards of white faces
on white pillows, between crisp white sheets.
The operating theatres are hung with icicles
of assorted pains, waiting for the patient to awake.

My friend has died. The sherpas are disheartened.
They chant mantras and won't carry my load.
They are removing the aluminium ladders. They
are packing. They burn incense to Chomolungma –
Goddess Mother Of The Land, whom I call Everest.
But I have seen the view from the Khumbu Glacier.
The white city is scaled. Already I am halfway up
the sky. The cautious ones, back at Base Camp,
seeing my headlamp, mistake me for a star.
I have to wear an oxygen mask, fight the sensation
that I have acquired a friend who eats half my rations,
creeps into my tent to make love to me nightly.

ICEFALL CLIMBING IN TIBET III

All night, snowflakes large as a father's hands stroked my face.
I crossed the glass sea of the Khumbu Glacier to be with you.
The icefall is crammed with the hotels you stayed in,
dragging wives, children, through mirrored halls, rooms
within rooms. You are the centre of each building –
the hardest core of ice. I have lived in homes perched
on a precipice. Each day more rooms broke off –
my mother is stepping out of the shower into the void.

Some blocks are packed with the beds of an orphanage.
We clung to our masts, adrift in a deepfrozen storm.
At the top of the icefall there's a serac I call the Prow.
After I've leapt over the crevasses in my memory,
trying to fill in the photos with you cut out –
my mother's scissors were silver as these icicles –
after I've crawled over your discarded towers, not daring
to peep in any of the windows, to see my half-sisters,
half-brothers, drowning in compacting ice –

I made it onto the Prow, that glass hulk, superliner
crashing over the icefall onto the sliding ocean.
I am scrubbing its deck because I want it to reflect me.
This ship is bearing a passenger I will not part with.
But father, you have not tricked me. Looking back,
I can find nothing in the icefall which is whole.
All the members of your family, from your mother
to my unborn children, are shaped like broken houses.

Their attics are blank. Their doors are closed,
if they have doors. Most of my relatives are mouthless
– who can talk to an absent father?
These abandoned cities are full of houses without doors,
without air – who can breathe in your glacial element?
So I leave the ship before it sets sail over the abyss.
The snow is crisp as sugar on the Western Cwm.
I can feel the black bones of the night under the skin of Everest.
I climb towards the highest point on earth, towards my father.

UNFREEZING THE SYV SÖSTRE

I did not expect it –
a palace falling, always falling from the cliff,
the rip of my mother's waters breaking.

To thaw is to let the thunder in,
the delirious torrent over my head,

to thaw is to shed my outer skin
leaving the new one raw

with its network of veins.
I am a complex of waterfalls.
I am one thousand feet tall.

All of me, every second,
is leaping out of the window,

all of my selves (those seven sisters)
somersault in the air

then hit rock.

THE FOREST GAME

Our family motto was Faithful to the Quiet Forests.

Mother said that if we were quiet
we'd hear what the trees were saying.

Children whose eyes are the colour of rain
should wear grey, she'd whisper.

Then her pupils would dilate
into two forest lakes

and she'd recite her special list –
temperate, deciduous, premontane, climax.

We sat rigid while she laughed seven times
which was the signal for the game to begin.

That night, my name was Dancing Stone
and my brother's was Homing Fish.

THE STRANGLER FIG'S STORY

My owner carried me to her bedroom,
told me I was her daughter
bought to cheer her up.

What I remember most were the nightly storms,
clouds descending from the ceiling
without relief of rain.

And I remember the voices in the clouds,
snow-crystals laughing
while she waited for me to speak.

The hours when everyone should be asleep,
even daughters obedient as plants

placed next to her and her cigarette.
Hours with burn-holes at their centre.

And the hour of her and the manicure scissors
snipping off half my leaves.

      ★

I waited for her to fall asleep.

I stole the oxygen in the room.

Then I turned to the body of my owner
and grew by the light of the moon.

From her breath I made rain.

From her darkness I formed the gloom of the forest,

drank her sweat as if it was dew,
the first morning of my future.

I fed on the dead cells of her skin,

sent out feelers to grip her clefts,
sprouted side and aerial roots.

I embraced her in a tight basket.

She withered slowly. In tree-time.

FOSSILING

The fossils are packed on top of each other
like children in dormitory bunkbeds.
Their sheets are wet. Nurses rub their noses in them.
It's the weekend, but my mother doesn't visit.

The gale is slapping me – the mother
who doesn't wish me to see her face
who had moods like this weather –
half the sky is on fire, half raining hailstones.

Between the undercliff and incoming tide,
giant ammonites are embedded in ledges
– a stone book with pages that take years to read,
stories of snakestones, devil's toenails . . .

★

This is just how it was, the slow petrification,
my core surrounded by a many-chambered shell
where I vacated rooms of selves.
The ocean pressing against my forehead.
The playground cruised by armour-plated fish.

Somewhere on the surface, a gale attacked me.
I felt nothing. The seas retreated,
were replaced by layers of stone seas.
Through cracks in the lias, voices filtered down.

Houses made of sand, shale, marl,
towerblocks, terraces, crushed together
and underneath, the ancestral house of mud.

The balcony fell into the sea
and there were floors where children were stranded,
floors so boggy we had to stay in bed,
knowing that when the voices upstairs
were raised, quicksands could swallow a child.

Bone-beds, shell-beds, stone-beds,
sheets cold as the skins of marine reptiles.

I sleepwalked down the coiled corridor,
passed doors leading to guardians' homes
– parents made of pyrite.

My thoughts were trapped in amber.
I began the long transformation of matter.

★

A boulder breaks open, releasing fossil ferns
– seven jewelled summers, when I drew
water from the wells of my bones
to keep Gran's garden from drying.

I climbed trees from the Coal Age
– giant clubmosses, horsetails,
and beyond the garden gate –
forests of peat, of anthracite;

the hollowed trunks of petrified trees
lined with amethyst, jasper.

On the blackboard, symbols recurred –
the mathematics of change, from leaf to fire . . .

Firemothers with magma in their veins,
babies that calcify in the womb
born with a stone guard in their hearts.

Daughters with the shells of trilobites,
forced to sleep in Cambrian slime,
feed on the debris of seafloors;
their skeletons on the outside,
rolled into a ball.

I uncurl the spirals of fossils,
unravelling stories buried inside me,
daughters that have to swim through stone.
The deeper I dig, the harder the child.

THE BOOK OF WATER

My mother is teaching me to swim.
Through the funnel of the whirlpool
I can see the aimara fish.
Father is fishing. Father Sun
dangle me from your hook
like a maggot, like a planet.
Breaststroke strengthens the heart
but I can't make the shallows,
my brother and I are in dangerous currents,
our parents have shut the bedtime book.
We sleep either end of the bed,
the story has reached our necks.

We wake in the maze of a delta.
O Rio Mar, your pages are written
by clouds of insects
which burrow into my flesh.
Your words hatch inside me
then eat their way out.
The ghost-trees of Solimoes
are flooded with silt.
I enter the river which flows backwards.
The source of the Amazon is in the sky.
I am a snowfish in the River of Rains,
my crystalline shape was spawned by the stars.
Before the Ucayali becomes the Apurimac
I leap up the Waterfall of Hope.
Sometimes life is a trickle,
sometimes life is a lake.
Some days are oxbows
best forgotten, except by the sloths.
The only humans this far upriver
are the Mayoruna
who drink frog-venom
and return to their past.

These days are so calm
dust floats on their surface.
A jaguar drinks at the edge of such moments.

Other days are blocked by mountains,
the spine of the Book of Water
is threaded with innumerable brooks.
Lord Oracle, Great Speaker
who carves prayer from stone
teach me the lingua velha.
There is a glacier to swim through,
a river of lava.
The sounds of children are settling
on the ultimate source
where the Incas have left them naked.
They sit and listen to the lake
on the cone of Mt. Mismi.
The water has flowed all around the world
before stretching icefingers
towards them, piercing them
like books never before opened,
the sun's fingers touching
their paperthin faces
and their inner pages –
tributaries of veins, forests of lungs
changed into icerivers, iceforests,
the central page of eggs and sperm
waiting like unwritten books,
twin-rivers intertwined in cells
– the alphabets of angels.

On the altar of Mt. Mismi
the sun is a father
who needs sacrifice.
He reels in his catch –
one son, one daughter.
His rays are colder than any knife.

The children give their souls to the sky
flying towards him as icebirds.
They sing the songs
of the Book of Earth,
the snows are their feathers.

THE MASSIF

My parents have always leant over me
with voices like thunder-rolls. They ask
where I've left my brother. As soon
as we entered, he insisted on swimming.

Was I supposed to hold the canoe in rapids,
whirlpools through which the riverbed gaped?
The Indians say that a thunderman
and thunderwoman live in the plateau,

that they capture souls to keep as children.
I've sensed the escarpment's walls
around each day, the way they're fissured
vertically and horizontally,

sensed also, beneath quartz sandstone
a foundation of granite. I've balanced
over the sinkholes of remembered conversations,
silences spanned by a lattice of roots

— unseen cataracts shook my bridges.
You were my echo — a brother of stone
whose words contained precious minerals.
A jasper creek is paved with your laughter.

Further up the canyon, where trees were draped
with epiphytes, the metal flowers
of a plane's fuselage warned pilots away.
I waded up a sunless gulche —

a green watersnake led me to a cave
its sole occupant, a fierce torrent
with spray like the snows in paperweights,
as if all our Christmases were pouring

into one family reunion. I wondered
if you'd been here, felt the draughts,
the concentric currents that drew and repelled,
each second stretching into a river.

Behind the falls, a narrow passage
led deeper into the mountain, down
streams laden with leaves large
as the letters we sent each other,

with the green ink of life, brown ink
of death, and all the shades of illness
in between, leaves that disintegrate
into the fulvic acids of blackwater

to merge with a sweetwater river
– Orinoco, Father-of-Rivers. There
the Water People sleep in stilt-huts
over the mangrove channels of a delta.

But here, at the source in this fortress
I cling to a legend told to me by Indians
– the magical appearance of windows
in the house of the thunders. On those days

clouds evaporate from the escarpment
and the windows open, releasing my brother.

SKINS

I am sewing the skins of birds end to end.
Snakeskins, woodskins, even the skin on water
must be dried, conserved, worn.
I am wearing my grandmother's spirits.
Her skin was rough from too much work –
I flay a tree, proof the bark for the river.
Her skin was soft from too much rain
but I cannot wear water.
So I have come to the world's loudest storm
to hear her sing. The sky-skin rips.
Her cheeks appear, wrinkled with lightning.

AUYAN TEPUY

Above the howls of the Araguato monkeys,
along cloud-forests of the lower slopes,
I follow the Churun river into Devil's Canyon.
I sleep in the cocoon of a mosquito net
beneath silk torrents. There are flowers
that open at night releasing Mother's perfume.

As if a mother is telling her daughter a story,
in her gauze négligé, her sheer dressing-gown
— I first catch sight of Churun Meru.
As I draw nearer, she talks faster, louder,
her face veiled by watersmoke.
As my mother talks, she turns from water to air.
Each drop of her is a waterworld or an airworld
I want to live in, enclosed in a rainbow-hoop
like the planet Saturn, canoeing up the sky-river
— surrounded by whirlpools of colour —
towards the sky-island which is home.

Gaps between floorboards wide as gorges.
Corridors with built-in cupboards like caves.
Wallpaper with leaves which eat children.
Our house has high ethereal winds.
I have to sit by my mother's bed.
She is a blackwater river full of acid.
She has been struggling with these rocks.
She will be the world's highest waterfall.
She twists and turns in her stone sheets
and nothing I say will soften them
or stop her falling into the canyon.

She carves me a stone uniform for her stone school,
teaches me the books of granite and sandstone,
how to sieve the book of water for gold,
how to read pages which keep changing –
pages teeming with piranha, pages that are mists.
The walls of our house have been eroded by water.
I crawl through those holes
down secret passageways into the understorey.
Some of the walls are decorated with leaves,
carnivorous species that survive our harsh climate.
I want to hide in the forest, dwarfed by buttresses.

Other rooms are filled with clouds.
Mother won't tell me what happens in those rooms.
I think my father lives there.
Once, I asked her what he looks like –
she said his eyes were long deep tunnels
full of silt, where his children are buried.
I climb into the root-mat of the wallpaper,
into a sinkhole where it is cool, quiet, dark
– the fossil heart of the forest, where the tree
which made my first breath can be carved into a canoe
for a journey into the undermountain.

I rescue the children buried in my father's eyes.
There are as many children as days in my childhood –
the infants who were learning to speak –
who hid in his mouth, under his tongue,
had just mastered the word Father, when he swallowed them.
There are children who entered his heart
along mineral-rich veins. I squeeze through a gorge
into the cave where a sister lies in his arms.
This is the last time he will see her.
His tears are diamonds embedded in granite.

I take the children I have rescued – sky-sisters,
sky-brothers, to the great Water-Falling-From-The-Sky,
Churun Meru, mother who guards our fortress
and I throw my childhood into the canyon.

*Auyan Tepuy is the Pemón Indian name for Devil's Mountain, a large tabletop
mountain in the Venezuelan Amazon. Churun Meru is the Pemón name for Angel
Falls, the world's highest waterfall, situated in Devil's Canyon, a long canyon leading
deep into the tepuy.*

BIRDWOMAN

What I remember of my grandmother is her face ready for sleep,
without glasses or teeth, her broken body at the bottom of the stairs,
tiny as a fallen nestling – I have come to this majestic bluff

to witness her last moment, the staircase blurred and incandescent
as this mile-high wonder plunging from the escarpment.
I set my trap lines and mist net between mahogany and kapok giants.

Nights, I'm busy in the skinning tent drying bird skins over the fire.
I've caught bellbirds, golden cocks of the rock, many hummingbirds.
Primaries, secondaries, tail-feathers for braking and landing,

bones hollower, lighter than the human, fused together for flex,
forward thrust, lifting force, gliding flight, momentum, impact.
I smoke all moisture from the birds then write in my journal:

November 6th, 6 a.m. Weak light, much cloud. During the dawn
    chorus
I watched a wing of water rise on a cushion of air above the main
    body,
pause long enough for a fledgling's feathers to break through the
    skin.

CLIMBING MOUNT RORAIMA

Tomorrow, instead of visiting my mother
I'll climb Mount Roraima.

The beast-father
has thrust a thorn through my tongue.

He's hung tapir-teeth around my neck,
stuck white breast-down
from king vultures in my hair.

He's sent his sky-jaguars
to rerape my mother, reconceive me.

They've left their traces
in silver waterfalls on rose quartz.

The sun drops behind the rim.
Fireflies signal *go, don't go.*

       ★

Crystal Mountain,
Mother of All Waters,

House Whispering of Waterfalls,
when your voices say *sororo* –

everyone must be quiet
to let the dead-names
of my father be remembered.

How does a blue soul turn red?

All night I lie in the swampy meadow
asking the moonlit wall.

I ask the rain
and the silver falls that appear before dawn
swell with the rain's answer.

I ask the sun's first rays
if it's time to play my bird-bone flute.

The real birds trill
just like my phone
when Mother rings,

just like my door
when no-one's there.

★

I wade through the domain of bushmaster
and saroroima snake.

I ascend the Ramp,
do not look left
at Roraima's neighbour – Suicide Mountain.

Nobody returns from that table-mount.
Nobody knows what meal-times were like,

how long I stared at the table surface
looking for a scratch to hide in.

No matter where I put my foot
or my hand or my face
it's always in the wrong place,

on a landslide of shale,
under a stinging torrent.

★

A mountain lioness, two cubs,
bar my way.

They've sprung from a cave
on the scent of my tapir-teeth necklace.

The torrent protects me
with its fierce veil.

I rest on top of the precipice,
to take out my gift –
an old letter from my mother:

. . . *you are my daughter, I'm sure
that deep down I do really love you.*

I read this out loud
in the grey place where voices echo.

I yell into the Gran Sabana
until the thunders stir in their pits.

Then I offer her letter to the winds.
It slaps my face
then is snatched away

to drift between Hell House
and the House of Angry Spirits.

I turn to my task.
The door is a slit between two boulders.

I pull myself into the white darkness
of the Fog Father and Mist Mother,

they touch me with icy fingers.

THE DOLL'S HOUSE

The doll's house is roofless, so I can fill it with sand.
I'm a giant making dunes ripple with my breath.

I sift a fine rain over my father, who's surprised
to be drowning in a dry sea. At last, he's quiet.

I can show visitors the courage it took
to cross the wilderness of our lounge,

my mother's twin suns burning into my head;
the cold nights, when even Berbers would have cuddled.

Mother is telling me to hoover. The dust is up to her neck.
But the bag's full and blows out tornadoes.

Father manages to burrow his way through to Algiers.
He craves open spaces. All he wants is to forget.

During long camel-rides, he sees mirages –
a bed shimmers on the horizon. His children are inside.

He rushes towards them but they sink back into the Sahara.
He finds his daughter's doll's house, the roof

ripped off by siroccos. She's grown up now.
He helps her dig the sand from the rooms.

THE BURNING

Bury me up to my neck
in the sands of my father's desert.

Down in the Great Emptiness
let the fire of his country

burn my face all day.
If I lose consciousness

revive me
only at night

with a sip of water from the Styx
and a sip from the Acheron,

bring me samples of all rivers
from the Old World and the New.

When my father finally appears,
moisten my mouth with a drop

from the Phlegethon – river of flames,
my thirst

will teach me the words
to draw him to me.

I'll breathe very deeply,
sucking the brown dust that is his flesh

into every inch of my lungs,
until there is no more of his power left on the earth.

Only then may you seal my lips with a thorn
to keep my soul-force in.

Other books in the same series include

KEVIN CROSSLEY-HOLLAND *Poems from East Anglia*

MARTYN CRUCEFIX *A Madder Ghost*

HILARY DAVIES *In a Valley of This Restless Mind*

DAVID GASCOYNE *Encounter with Silence*

DAVID GASCOYNE *Selected Prose 1934-1996*

GARY GEDDES *Flying Blind*

PHOEBE HESKETH *A Box of Silver Birch*

JEREMY HOOKER *Our Lady of Europe*

NICKI JACKOWSKA *Lighting a Slow Fuse*

JUDITH KAZANTZIS *Swimming Through the Grand Hotel*

BLAKE MORRISON & PAULA REGO *Pendle Witches*

VICTOR PASMORE *The Man Within*

MYRA SCHNEIDER *The Panic Bird*

ANTHONY THWAITE *Selected Poems 1956-1996*

EDWARD UPWARD *Remembering the Earlier Auden*

EDWARD UPWARD *The Scenic Railway*

Please write to Enitharmon Press for a full catalogue